123

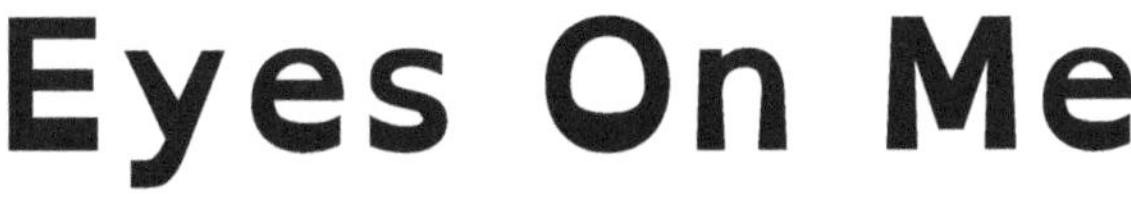

Eyes On Me

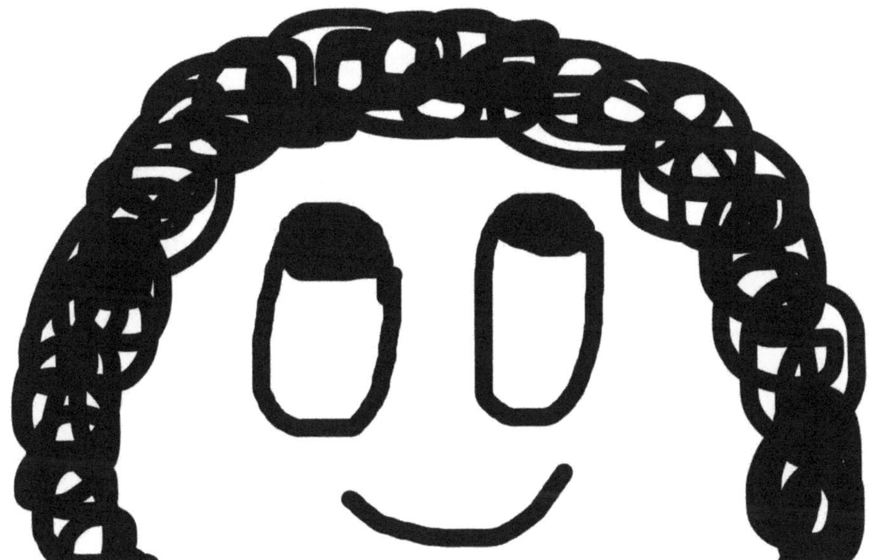

Written & Illustrated By: Emily Moon

© 2025 by Emily Moon

All rights reserved. No part of this publication may be reproduced, distributed or transmitted in any form or by any means, including photocopying, recording, or other electronic or mechanical methods, without the prior written permission of the publisher, except in the case of brief quotations embodied in critical reviews and certain other noncommercial uses permitted by copyright law. While all attempts have been made to verify the information provided in this publication, neither the author nor the publisher assumes any responsibility for errors, omissions, or contrary interpretations of the subject matter herein. Adherence to all applicable laws and regulations, including international, federal, state, and local governing professional licensing, business practices, advertising, and all other aspects of doing business in the US, Canada, or any other jurisdiction is the sole responsibility of the purchaser or reader. Any perceived slight of any individual or organization is purely unintentional.

ISBN: 979-8-9939565-0-3
heymrsmoon.com

Dedicated to: Mom and Julia

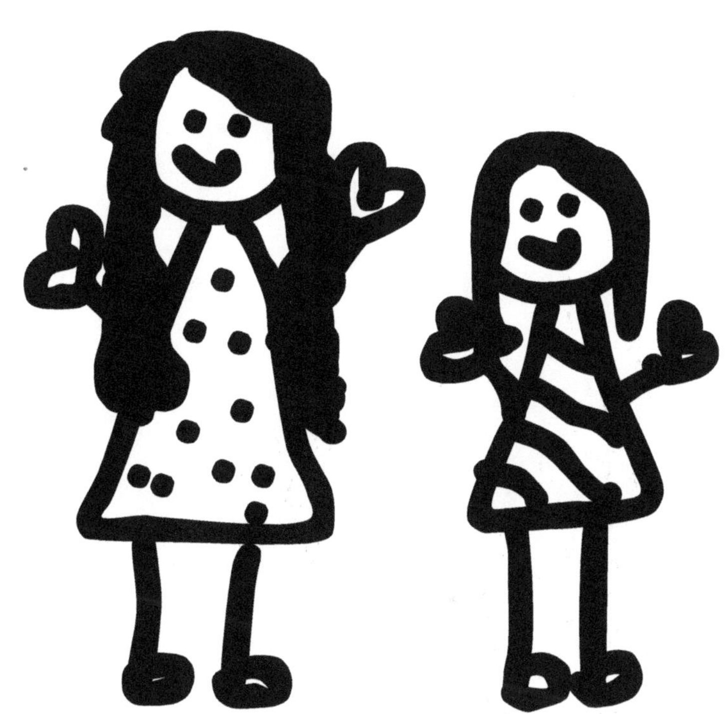

Look to Jesus, the founder and
perfecter of our faith, who for the
joy that was set before him endured
the cross, despising the shame,
and is seated at the right hand of
the throne of God.

-Hebrews 12:2 ESV

When the sun comes up for a brand new day, I hear God say,

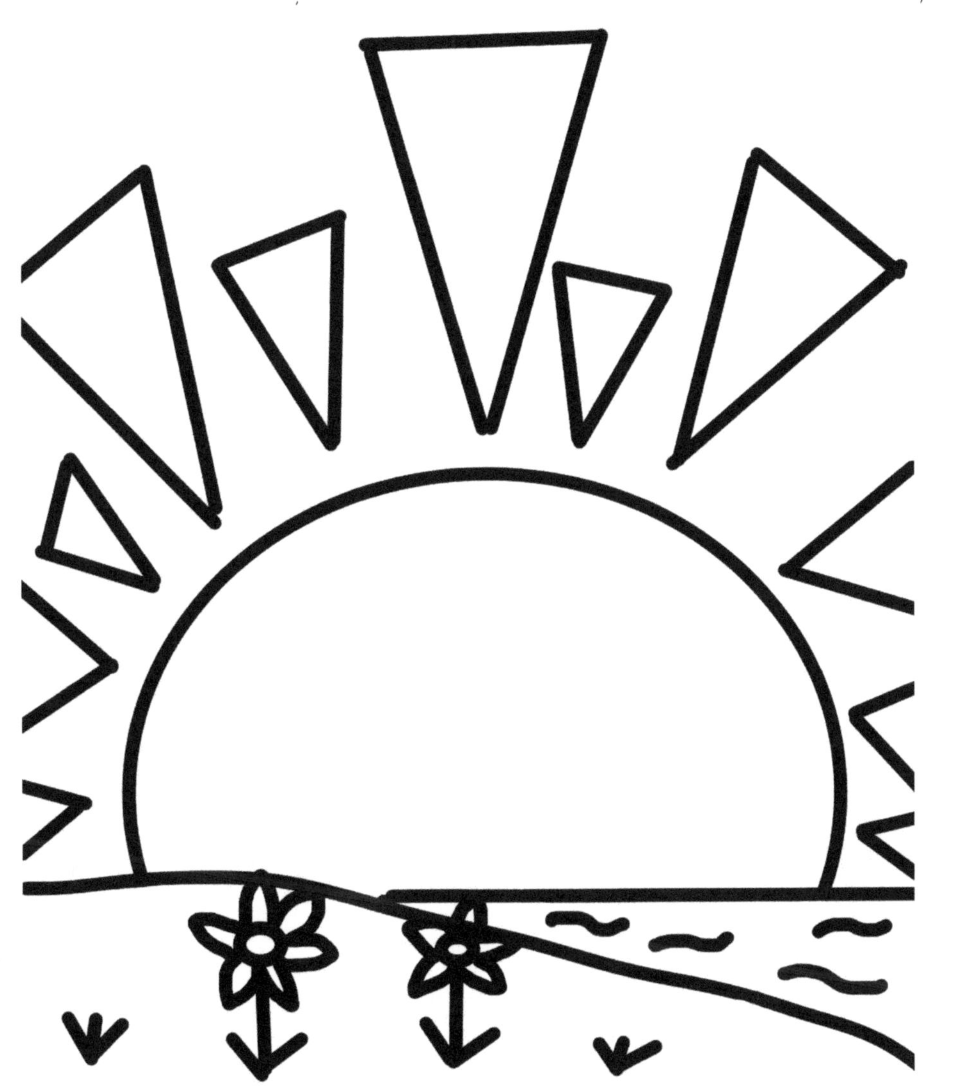

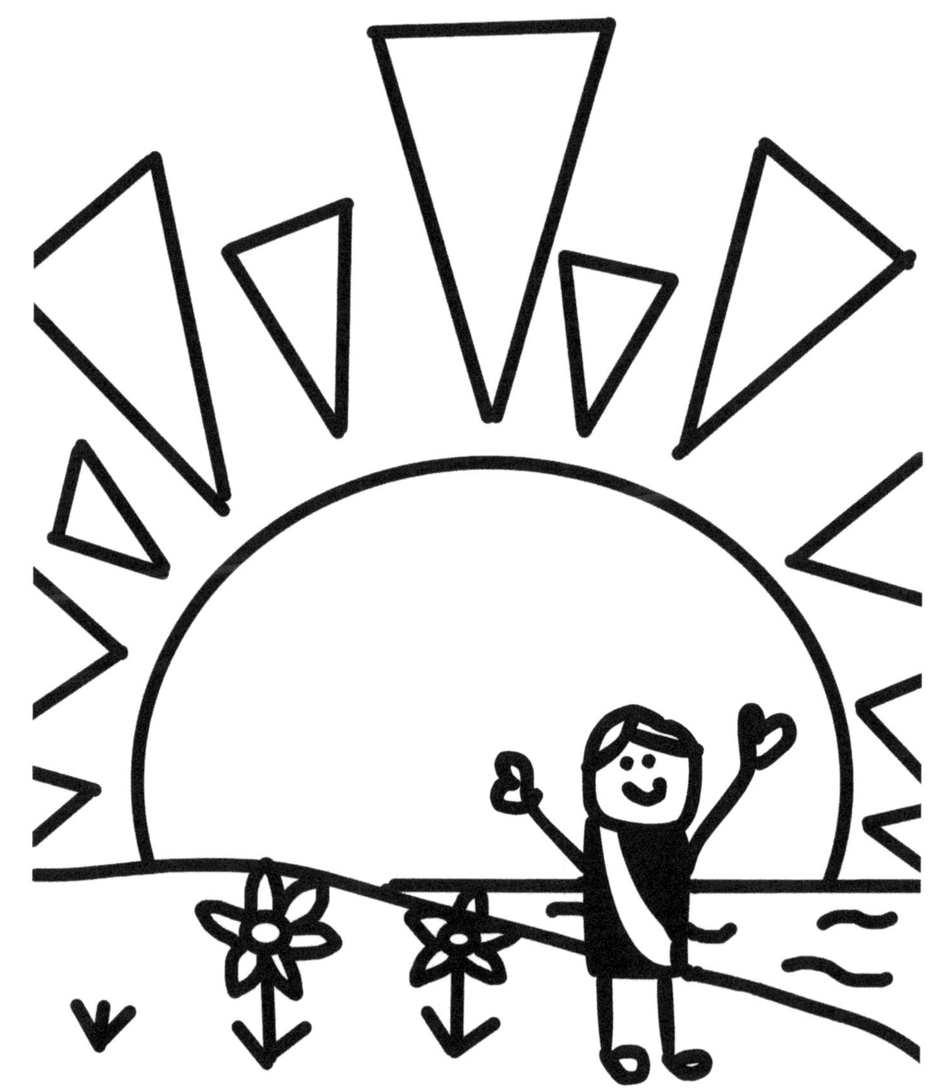

"123 eyes on Me!"

When it is time to eat, I thank God for the treat!

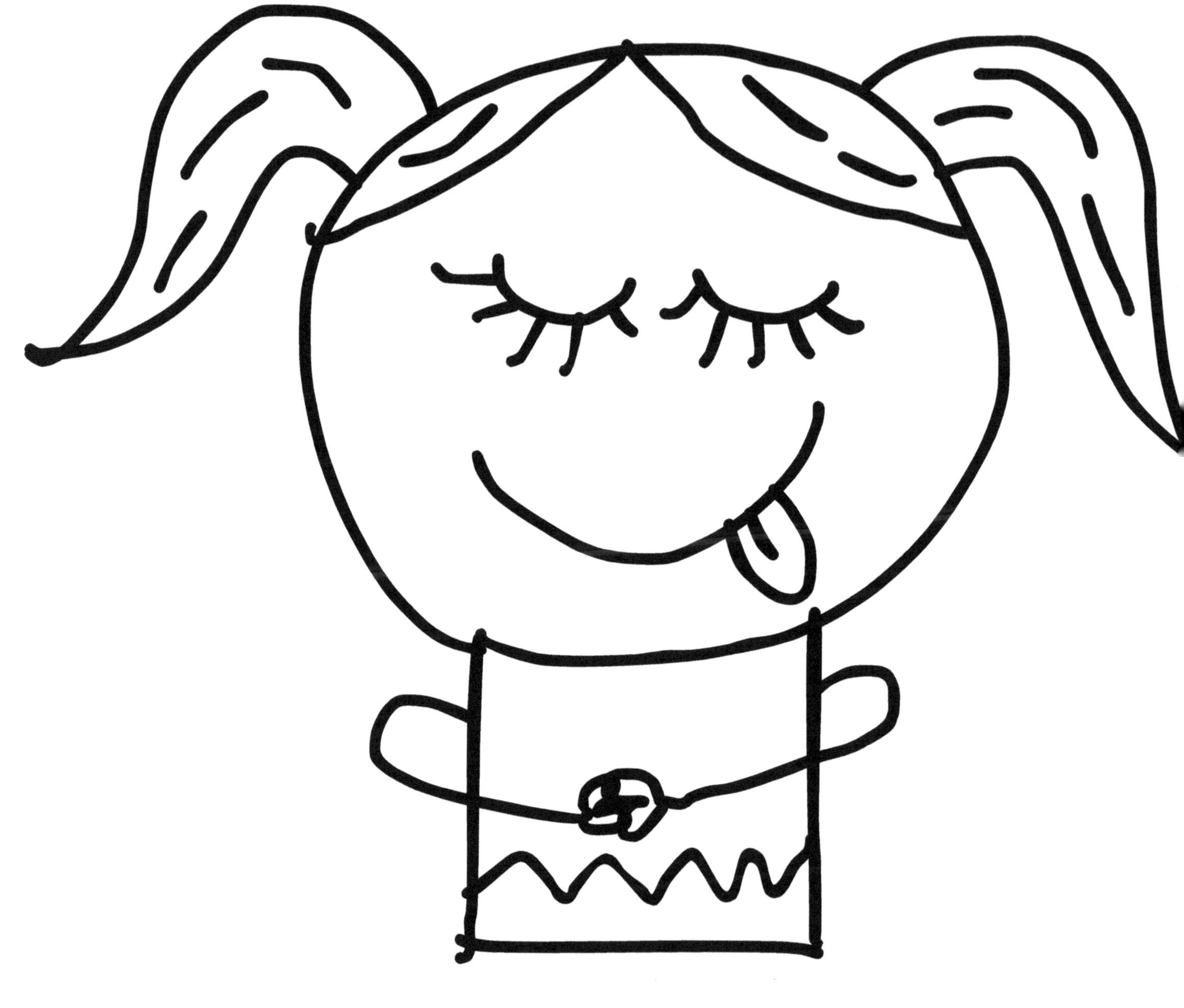

"123 eyes on Me!"

When we go for a trip in the car,
God is never too far.

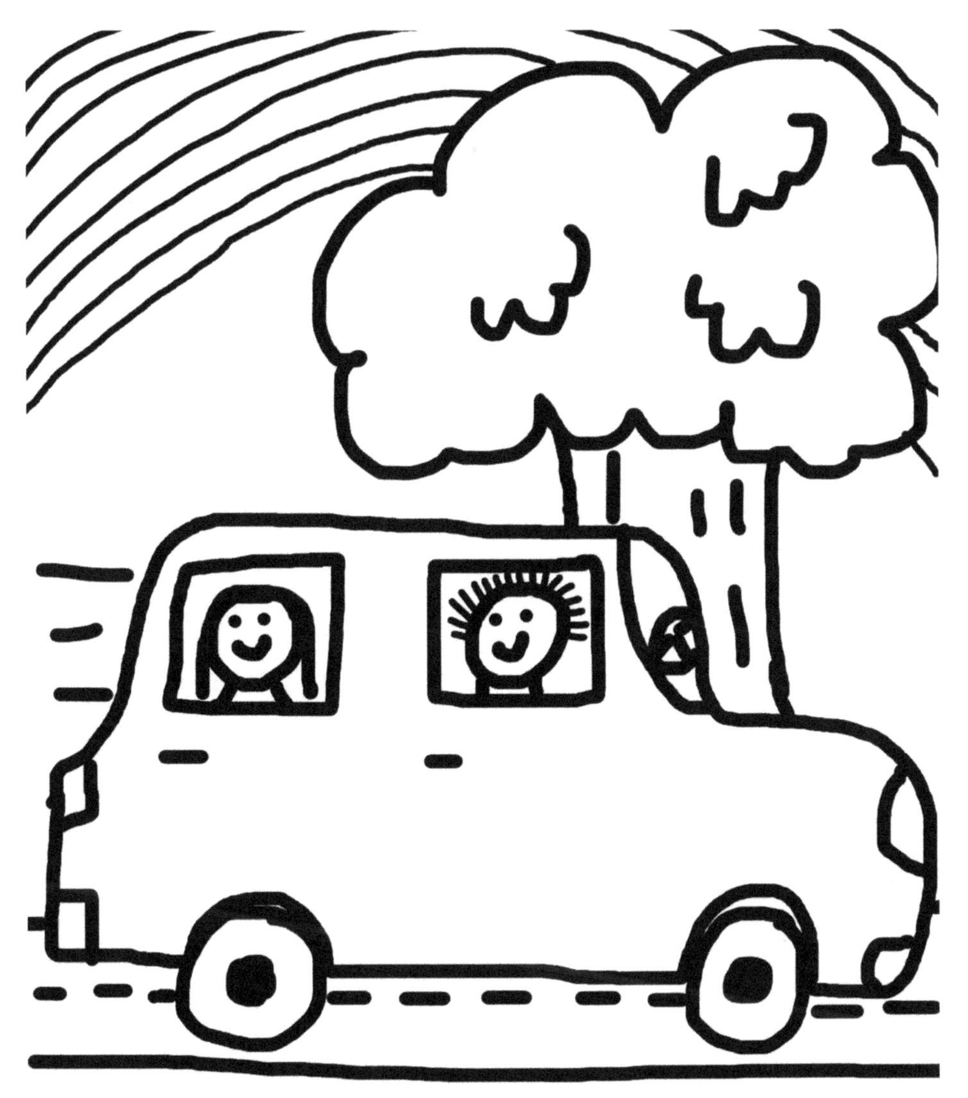

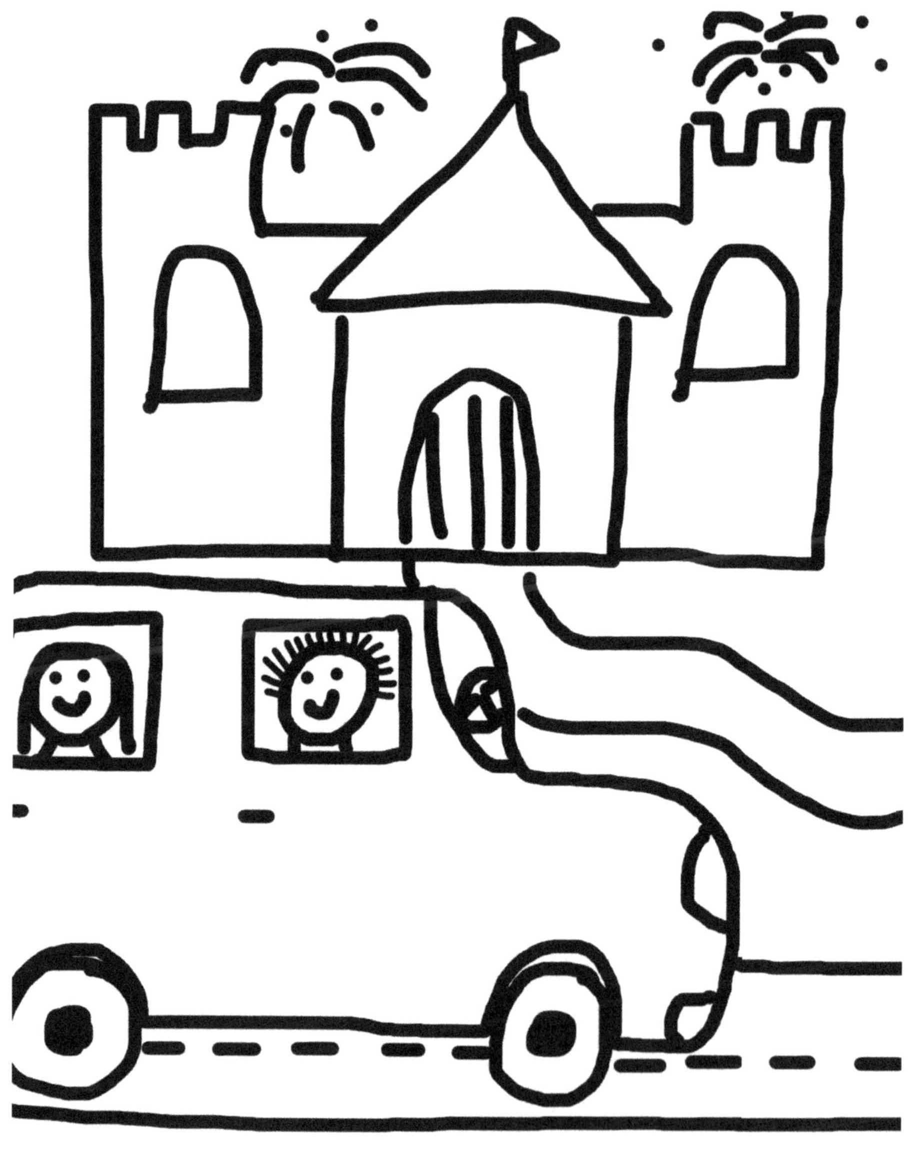

"123 eyes on Me!"

When I get scared,

I know God cares.

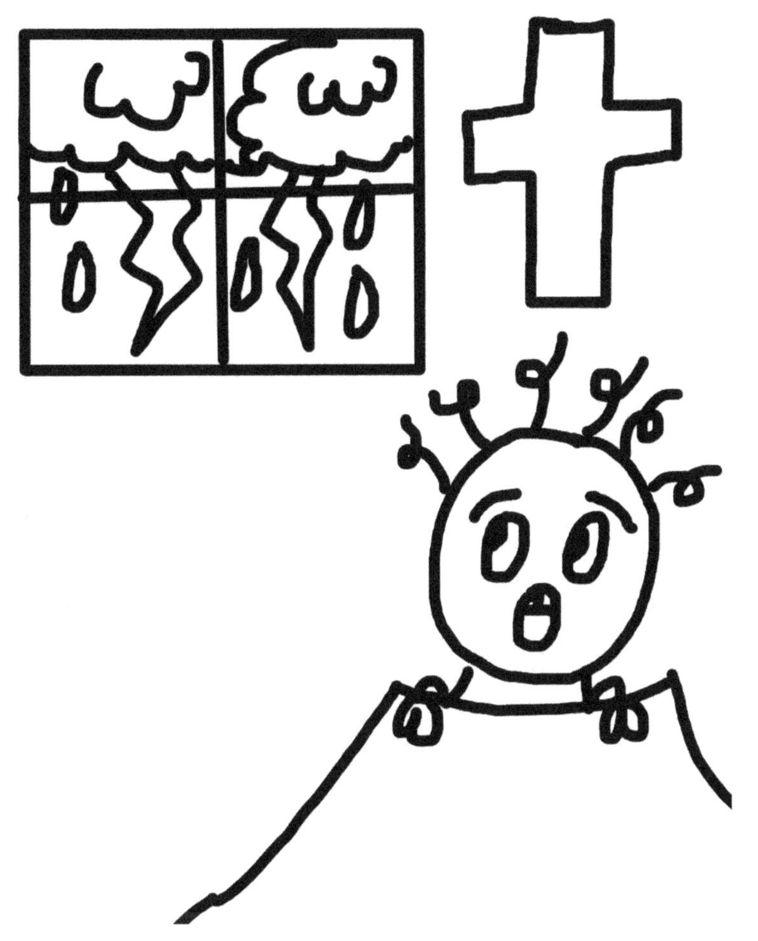

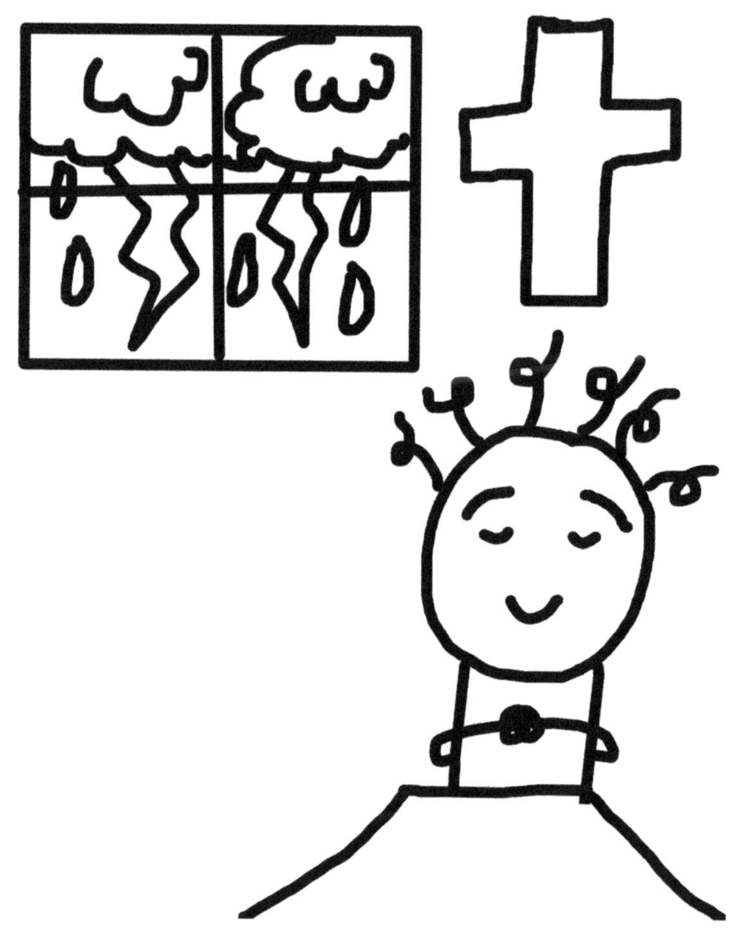

"123 eyes on Me!"

When I'm at school and don't know

what to do,

what God says is true.

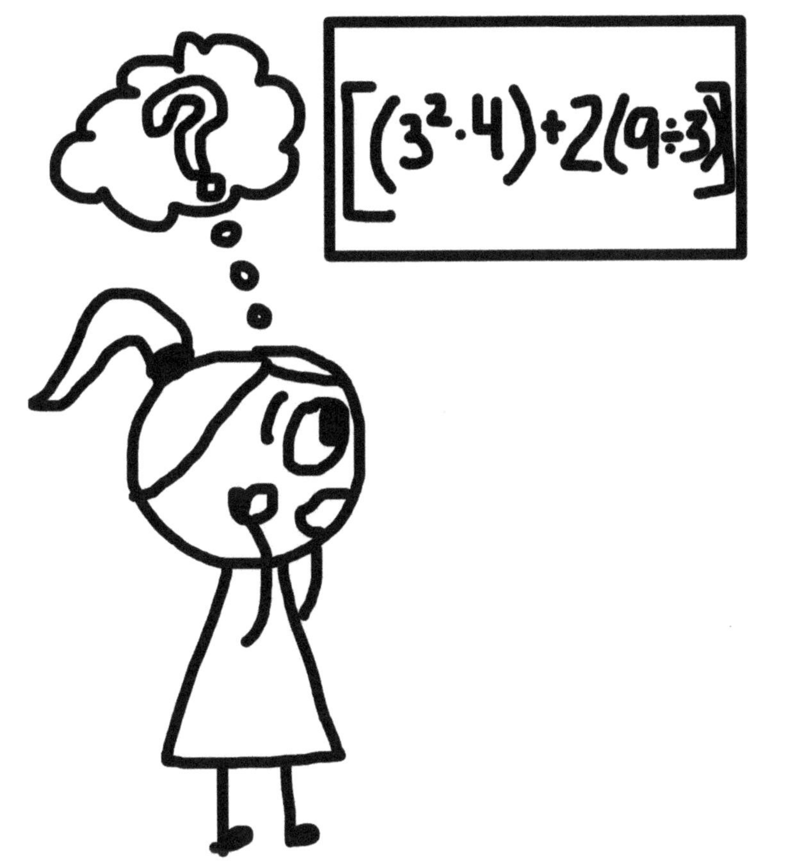

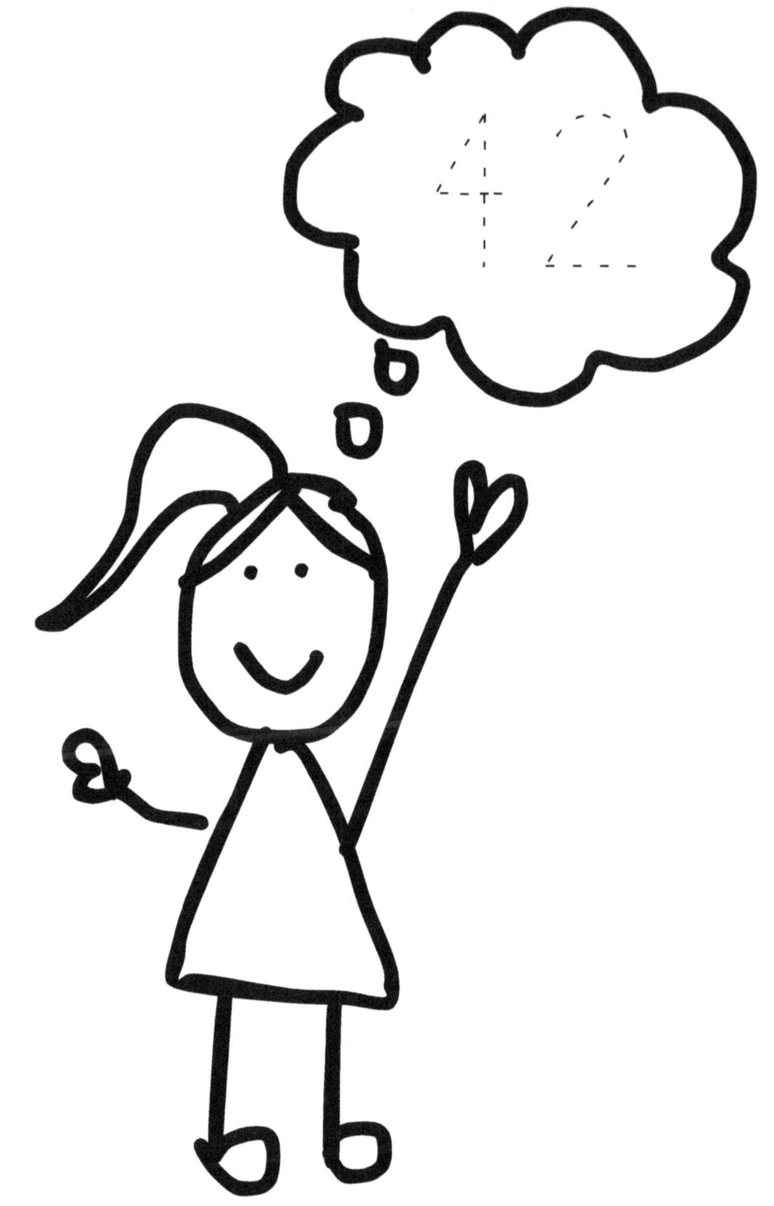

"123 eyes on Me!"

When I need to be brave, but don't know if I can, God takes my hand.

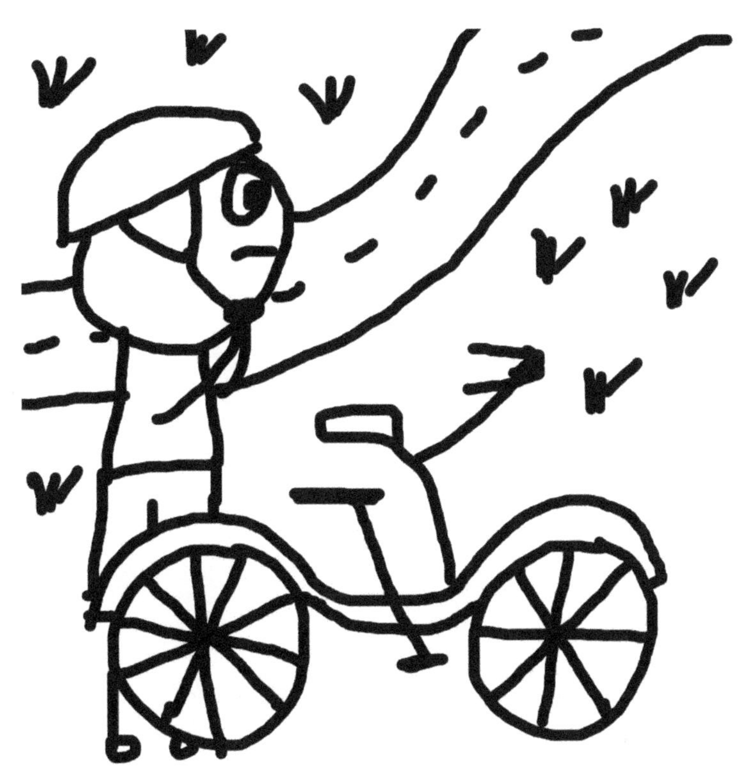

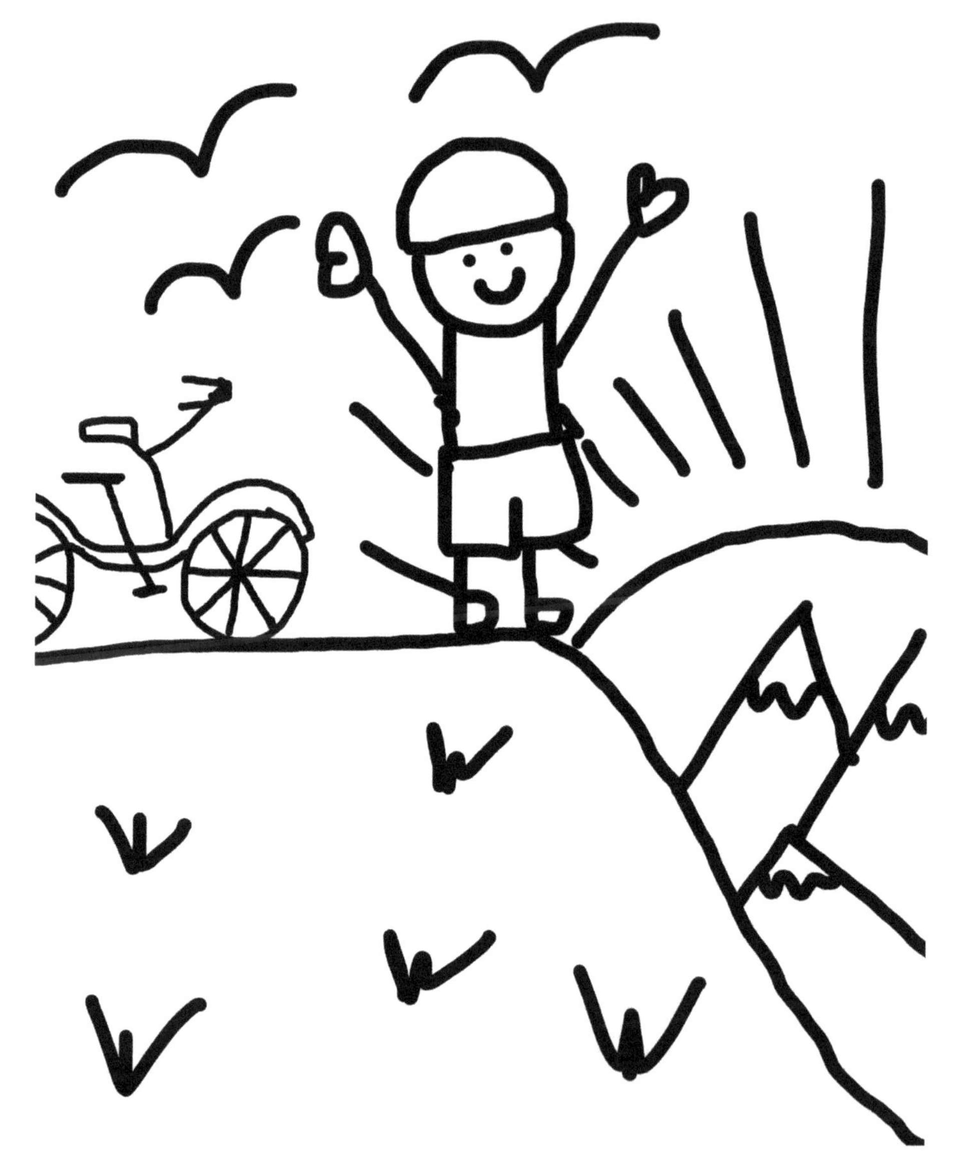

"123 eyes on Me!"

When I am as happy as can be,

I thank God for blessing me.

“123 eyes on Me!”

No matter what comes my way,
with me I know God will stay.

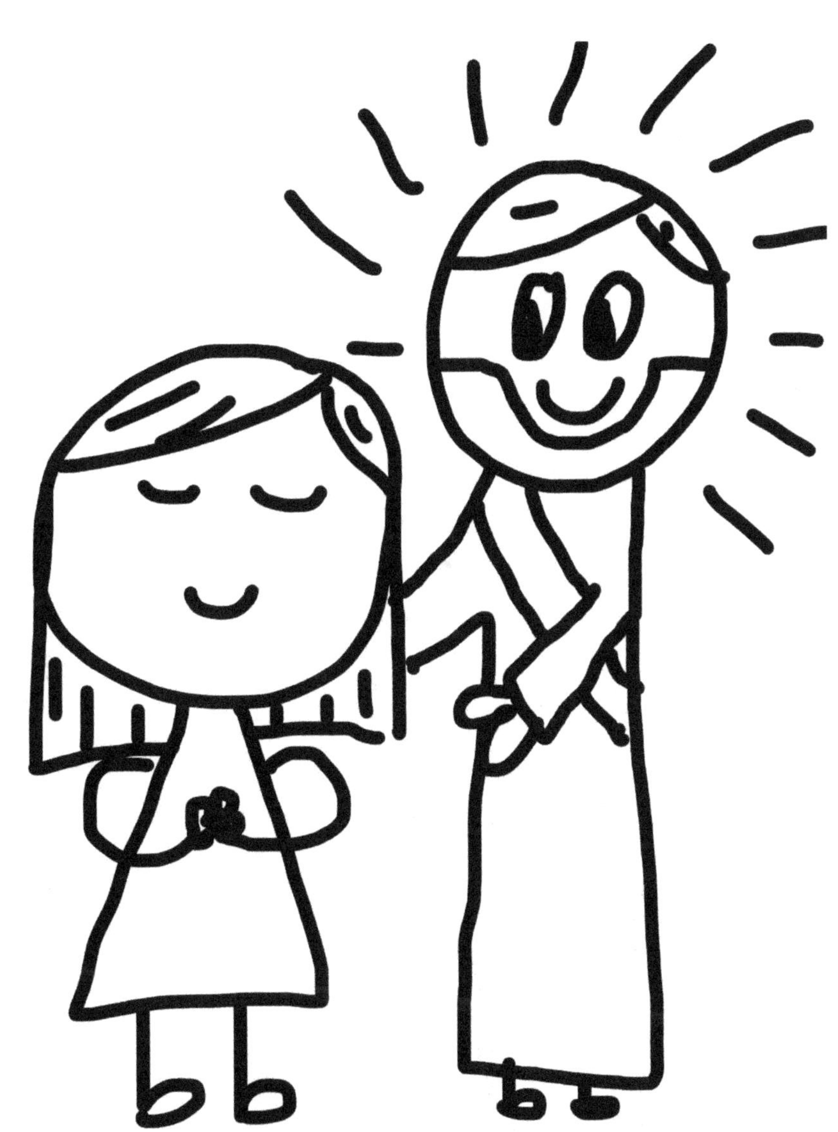

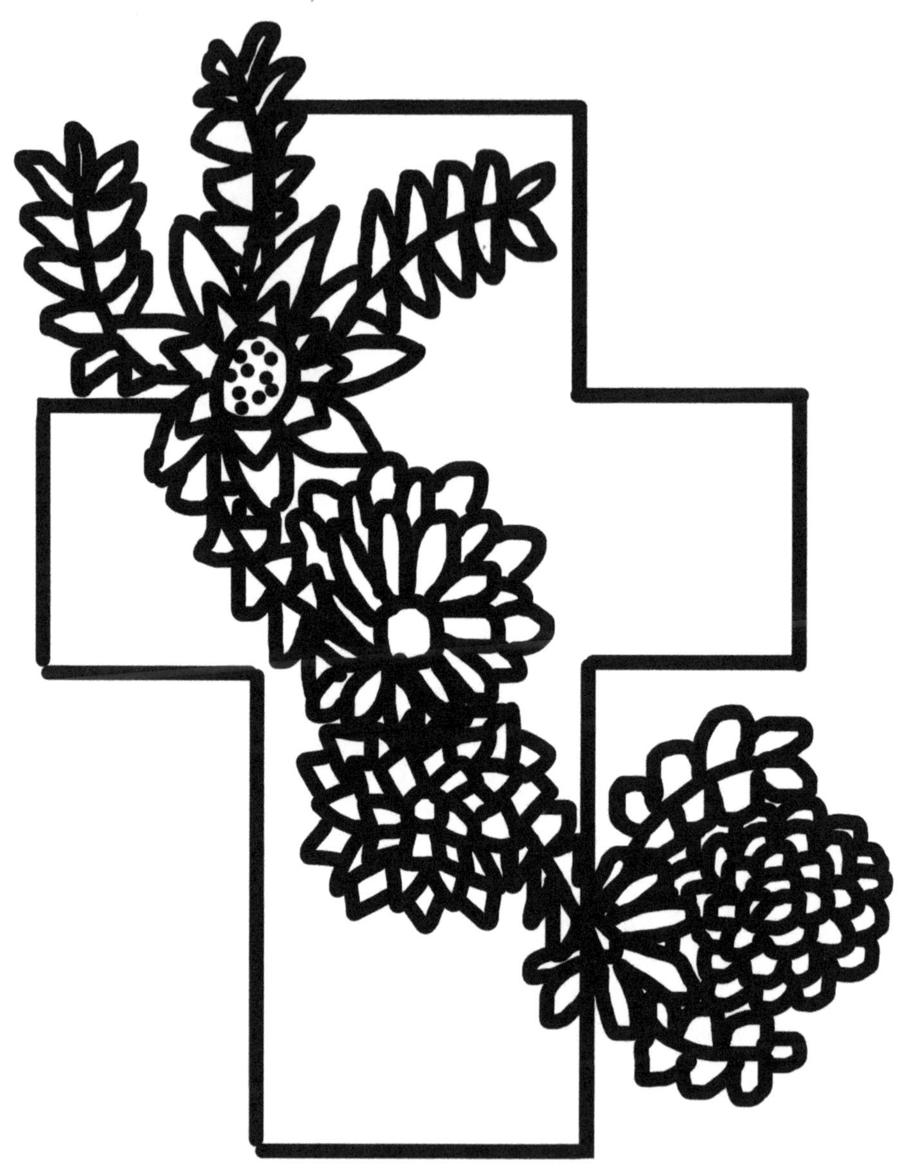

“ 1 2 3 God’s got me!”

heymrsmoon

www.ingramcontent.com/pod-product-compliance
Lightning Source LLC
LaVergne TN
LVHW070933160826
845679LV00018B/1788